Min

A DIVINE DETOUR

FROM DOCTORATE
TO DIAGNOSIS TO DESTINY

*Love,
Taleshia
Chandler*

TALESHIA L. CHANDLER, PH.D.
(FOREWORD BY DR. CHARLES E. BOOTH)

Cover art designed by Kingdom Graphic Design, LLC.

FIRST EDITION

ISBN: 978-0-9976982-1-3

Library of Congress Control Number: 2016946702

Published by

Certa
PUBLISHING

P.O. Box 2839, Apopka, FL 32704

Printed in the United States of America

Disclaimer: The views and opinions expressed in this book are solely those of the author and other contributors. These views and opinions do not necessarily represent those of Certa Publishing.

࿇

---

*In Memory of Aunt Brenda
and my grandfather,
Elder Norwood E. Gross, Sr.*

Dedication

I dedicate this book to every intercessor who has called my name out to God. During the days that I was too weak, too sad, too angry, and too afraid to speak, I believe God heard your prayers. Prayer has been the road map to guide me to a doctorate, through a diagnosis, and onward to my destiny!

Table of Contents

Special Thanks

God, thank You for always keeping Your promises. Thank You for being so faithful to me throughout this process and throughout my life. You are my Jehovah Rapha. Thank You for healing me ... again. I give You all of the glory, and I'm going to tell everyone what You've done for me!

To my amazing husband, Anthony, for being my biggest supporter and encourager. Thank you for being so patient. I could not have made it through any of this without your love and constant support. Thank you for covering our house, my priest. I'm still counting the stars, forever and always! I love you so much, Baybey!

To my three incredible children, Anthony II, Alysha, and Andrew, who inspire me every day and allow me to see my true purpose in life. I love you guys more than you'll ever know. I pray that each one of you will fulfill your destiny and be all that God has created you to be!

To my mom, Judy, for being my prayer warrior. I know that I'm alive today because of you. Not only because you gave birth to me, but every time it felt like my life was going to end, I know you went before God, as my personal intercessor, and then, commanded the devil to leave me alone. I love you, Mom!

To my dad, Lee, for encouraging me to (well, actually making me!) sing. I love you, Dad!

To my sister, Tabitha, for being the best sister ever! You helped me stay awake through the writing of my thesis and dissertation. You have traveled to spend time with me and never missed any of my cancer treatments. You are one of the funniest people I know. I love you, Sista!

To my brothers, Lee and Rodney, for your love and many texts that keep me laughing. I love you guys!

Grandma Lucy, you are my hero. I can stand tall because I'm on your shoulders. I love you!

To my Mother Boobie Dear, Queen, thanks for being more than a mother in-*love* but one of my closest friends. We just get each other. I love you to pieces lady!

Ms. Pat, thank you for all of the sidesplitting laughter. You are my sister-mother-friend.

To my special group of sister-friends, "GA," for keeping me smiling and laughing. You give me something to look forward to every day. Thank you. I love you gals for life!

To Tamara, thank you for being a consistent friend and awesome resource throughout this ordeal.

To my brother, Eric, for always looking out for me!

To Big Brother Vernon for an awesome title!

To my posse (Sandra, Henrietta and Dellyse), you will always have a special place in my heart. I love you gals!

To Natasha, Karol, Alan, and my husband for reading my drafts and helping me with the writing process, you all are so smart!

To Martina and Tony Turner at Unleashed Salon. You don't just do hair, but you minister to your clients. Thank you for making me feel pretty again!

To my colleagues at RPS, who donated hours and held me down during my leave of absence. Thank you so much for your generosity!

To my entire family and all of my friends. Thank you and I love you all!

To my Cedar Street Church Family, thank you for your prayers and support. Thank you for embracing my family and me and for taking care of us. I love you!

⚜

Acknowledgements

Dr. Arcella Trimble and Dr. Sandra Harris, you were beyond patient with me during our eight-year journey at Walden. Thank you for not giving up on me.

Dr. Joseph Evers and the awesome staff at the Virginia Cancer Institute, you renewed my faith in health care providers and nursed me back to good health. I pray that God will continue to use you to minister to other cancer patients with the same professionalism and compassion you have given me. Thank you for helping me on my detour!

First Lady Karen Clark Sheard, thank you for inspiring me not only through your music, but also through your beautiful spirit, your prayers, and mentorship. I have been following your ministry for over thirty years, and you have blessed my life tremendously. I feel honored to call you my mentor and sister-friend. I love you dearly!

Dr. Charles Booth, Bishop Oscar and Lady Jacqueline Brown, Bishop Walter Scott Thomas, Bishop Michael Dantley, Drs. Ann and Stanley Fuller and so many other outstanding pastors who've prayed for me and my family. Thank you for your leadership!

Foreword

A cross the broad span of the years, transparency has not been in vogue. I am a part of a generation which taught concealment, especially when the reality was uniquely personal and painful. However, we now live in a generation where individuals have emerged from the closet of concealment and now inhale the fresh air of open truth, regardless of how painful and personal that truth may be.

Dr. Taleshia L. Chandler has emerged from such a closet and out of the pain of her predicament. She, like Job, speaks with boldness from the mat of a misery that now belongs to the not too distant past. She and I share a common bond, for I, like she, have emerged from the long journey of cancer acknowledgment, to the place where we both can say with triumph— *"I can do all things through Christ who strengthens me."*

There are no more dreaded words than those, which fall from the lips of the physician— "You have cancer." At first blush, one thinks this is a death sentence or *"Why is this happening to me?"* or *"Is God punishing me for something thought, said or done?"* Dr. Chandler eloquently and honestly speaks from her hurt, revealing the true treasure of her pilgrimage during this dark season of her journey. She is to be commended for her honesty. In so sharing her odyssey through this ordeal, Dr. Chandler personifies the reality of which our Lord spoke when He declared, "Truth shall make you free" (John 8:32). The truth of Christ has become the truth of this lady's faith, and such truth has released her to inspire all of us on our journey to overcome the darkness that would seek to consume us.

This woman of faith has chronicled for us a wonderful work of inspiration and hope. I encourage all to read these pages and sift from these leaves the mountains Dr. Chandler has climbed, as well as the valleys through which she has trod. True faith, healing, and deliverance can only come when we blend the highs and lows of our journey. Out of this synthesis emerges true faith!

Lady Chandler has encouraged me in my continuing battle against the demon of cancer. In the reading of her work, I am determined in my fight, as you will be in yours, knowing that light will always conquer darkness, and victory comes to those who hold unflinchingly to the Christ who said, "Lo, I am with you always even unto the end of the world" (Matthew 28:20). Lady Chandler would have us to know that detour does not mean deterrent, because detour really means determination—the determination to run this race with patience, "Being confident of this very thing, that he who hath begun a good work in you will perform it until the day of Jesus Christ" (Philippians 1:6).

Dr. Charles E. Booth, *Senior Pastor*
Mt. Olivet Baptist Church ~ Columbus, Ohio

Introduction

I was prepared to celebrate one of the happiest years of my life. I had celebrated my fortieth birthday and became friends with one of my favorite people on the planet. My oldest child was in his senior year of high school. After a rocky start, he was accepted to a four-year program. After an eight-year stint of study, and what appeared to be academic torture, I was finally nearing the end of my doctoral studies program. I had a job that put my foot in the door for some great opportunities in education.

I thought, wow, God, everything is just perfect! My marriage is secure, my children are all excelling in school, I love my church, and I am so proud of the work that my husband is doing as a pastor. I feel that we are making a positive difference in our community. I am far from perfect, but I believe that you are pleased with the way that I live. After all, I don't curse, smoke, or drink. I just like my roulette and a winning number every now and then (Don't judge me!). I'm a tither, so that really shouldn't matter, right? I am a good steward of my time, talent, and tithe. I absolutely love to spread joy and visiting the sick to spread love and Your message of hope. What could possibly go wrong?

It was Women's Month and as first lady of the church, I was involved in the planning and execution of every church activity for the entire month of May. We kicked off with some great activities and worship experiences. By the third week, I had a hard fall on one of the pews in church and began experiencing excruciating back pain. I, automatically, associated the pain with the fall, despite the fact that I previously had some questions and concerns for my doctors.

Unlike some previous ailments, it just seemed as if this pain wasn't going away. It hindered my daily functioning, and no matter what I tried, it just wouldn't go away. I tried emergency medicine, chiropractic care, physical therapy, medication, massage therapy, personal training, and orthopedic care and NOTHING worked! After all of these failed attempts, I was finally allowed to have an MRI. On result day, I heard the words that no one wants to hear at any medical appointment, "You need to see an oncologist."

I asked God, "Am I being punished?" "Do you still love me?" Why would you give me everything—the man of my dreams, three wonderful children, a doctorate, a career, friends, and happiness, just to take it all away?" I proceeded to tell Him, "I'll do whatever you tell me to do. Please just take this one thing away and let me finish enjoying all that you have given me. It's not fair, and I don't understand why you would punish me so harshly. I see others doing things far worse than I do, and they aren't sick, not like this."

God, why me?

≪≫

CHAPTER 1

Higher Learning

My people are destroyed for lack of knowledge.
—Hosea 4:6a

Since growing up in Northwest Baltimore, I've always had a passion for learning and teaching. My love for learning lasted throughout grade school, where I consistently maintained honor roll status. After I completed my undergraduate studies, I was an elementary school teacher for about ten years, and then, I decided to pursue a master's degree. It was difficult managing a household of three children, being a pastor's wife, and working full-time, but I was determined. I earned my master's degree in two years. My ultimate academic dream was to earn a doctorate in psychology, with a specialization in education.

In order to achieve my goal, I found an accredited program, which gave me the flexibility of distance learning and a quarterly face-to-face component to learn from my professors and socialize with schoolmates (who were also mostly balancing academics and family life). As an online student, I worked extremely hard. My workload included long reading sessions and lengthy writing assignments. I decided to pursue an educational psychology degree, to appease my love of education and to have a better understanding of how people learn and think. The courses were tedious, yet I was able to navigate through the coursework in two years with a 4.0 grade point average.

I had finally made it to the dissertation stage and looked forward to graduating within one year. However, this stage of the process took much longer than I expected. First, I had to think of a study that was feasible. (I suggest to anyone pursuing a doctorate, choose a topic and receive approval early on in your program of study!). It took one full year before I had an approved topic to begin my research. I then had to find a substantial amount of previous studies to support the need for my study, as well as the theory that grounded my study. It felt as though it took another year, or more, to read articles and summarize the main findings of other researchers.

By the end of my program, I'd read more than one hundred articles about inclusion in public schools and other topics related to my area of study. Carving out time to read and write became very challenging. My best option was to devise a very specific schedule to read, summarize articles, and write the chapters. I was fortunate enough to have a very thorough, yet compassionate, committee chair who helped me navigate the dissertation process. However, it was still my responsibility to do the leg-work, and it took seven years for me to read, research, and write what should have taken me less than one year to complete.

When I completed each chapter, I had to submit it for approval from my chair and methodologist separately. They each had two weeks to return my submissions, often with numerous corrections. I became discouraged each time, and it felt as though I would never finish. In addition to writing the chapters, I had to find a school district that was willing to participate in my study. And just as soon as I had found one, our family had to relocate to another state for my husband's new job. This was my first detour, but I was excited about this shift in the plan. Therefore, I had to find another school district for my study in order to have access to active principals.

Once I secured new participants, I went through a series of challenges with writing my document. At one time, I had so many documents that I had to spend a day to determine my most up-to-date manuscript to use for my writing sessions. When I became organized, I used most of my free time developing my draft. One by one, I began to make progress on each chapter of my document. I cried after each "yes" from my dissertation committee! Each "yes" put me a step closer to earning my doctorate. However, I also cried after each "no," each redo, and every edit, because my process seemed delayed. Thankfully, not every delay means a denial!

After eight years of reading, writing, editing, and revising, I finally had a completed and approved document. My oral defense was set for December 2014. I was on a timeline to successfully defend and have my document approved by the provost, in order to participate in the winter commencement set for January 2015 in Orlando, Florida.

In faith, I registered for the graduation ceremony and my husband booked flights and rooms. I was so determined to finish. I knew God had not brought me that far in the program only to keep me from crossing the finish line. And, just like He had done so many times, God showed up just when I needed Him the most! I successfully defended my study, received approval from my provost, and received clearance to graduate.

Walking across the stage to be hooded, and being addressed as, "Dr. Taleshia Chandler" was one of the highlights of my life. The fact that my husband, children, parents, and a few close friends, traveled to witness the ceremony, made the moment all the more special for me.

> Walking across the stage to be hooded, and being addressed as, "Dr. Taleshia Chandler" was one of the highlights of my life.

I was ready to move forward with my career and excited about new opportunities and possibilities, now that I had finally achieved my academic goals. I had my plan all mapped-out, and I was extremely excited about my future. School was behind me, and my destiny lay ahead! However, my plan did not completely play out as I had expected.

Lessons Learned

- *It's never too late to pursue your dreams.*
- *Write a plan that includes a specific timeline.*
- *Find the right people to help you achieve your goals.*
- *Celebrate the small victories along the way.*
- *Don't panic at every "no".*
- *Delays are not denials.*
- *Be open to detours, because God's plan is always much better than anything that we could ever think or imagine.*

All I Know

All I know is that God will be with you,
fight for you, and give you the victory
—Deuteronomy 20:4 NIV

〜❧〜

CHAPTER 2

The Diagnosis

But He was wounded for our transgressions, He was
bruised for our iniquities: the chastisement of our peace
was upon Him; and with His stripes we are healed.
—Isaiah 53:5

I began to look for new career opportunities. Simultaneously, I started to feel some aches and pains, which I'd never felt before. They would come and go, but I just knew that it was nothing serious. After all, I always kept my annual appointments and physicals, and my doctors assured me I was doing well. I just needed (and wanted) to lose a few pounds. So, I started to work out with a personal trainer. Occasionally, I would feel a sharp pain in my chest, but I thought that perhaps I was pushing myself too hard. I continued to look for a new job, as I worked on becoming more physically fit. Now that my schedule was free from reading articles and writing, I had no excuse to skip the gym.

Then the chest pain seemed to occur more frequently. I noticed that I felt the chest pain even when I hadn't worked out. During one of my weekly visits to the hair salon (which I soon discovered was a luxury I took for granted), I noticed that I felt an awkward ache in my chest when lifting up from the shampoo bowl. I started to become more and more concerned about what was going on with my body.

One of my biggest fears, for as long as I can remember, has been to receive a cancer diagnosis. Fear crippled me, to the point that I would adjust the volume or change the channel on any commercial or program related to cancer. For years, I had anxiety at every doctor's visit. This fear escalated after losing my aunt to colon cancer (at age forty-five) and my grandfather to prostate cancer. I refused to watch any movie or television show that involved any form of cancer in the plot. I couldn't even watch Oprah's shows about cancer!

> One of my biggest fears, for as long as I can remember, has been to receive a cancer diagnosis.

I started getting mammograms at age thirty-nine, as recommended by my doctor. I cried as soon as I entered the office for the first time, because I was so fearful at the thought of receiving a negative report. I researched radiology labs to determine where I could receive same-day results. I learned early, as an educated patient, I have the right to access certain options in my healthcare, but I had to do my homework.

At my first mammography, the radiologist informed

me that I have dense breast tissue and would always need an ultrasound in addition to the traditional mammogram. The radiologist asked me to return in six months, in lieu of the usual one-year turnaround, when things are normal. He said I had a visible lymph node on my film, and this made me quite uneasy. However, the doctor released me to the normal one-year schedule after my six-month follow-up.

Three months before my yearly mammogram was scheduled, I visited my gynecologist for my annual appointment. I informed her that during my self-checks, I noticed that my right breast felt different. She agreed and stated that she would review my most recent mammography reports. In her follow-up, the doctor stated that what she felt in the office was consistent with the radiologist's reports. Therefore, she told me to keep my scheduled mammogram appointment, in lieu of seeing the radiologist sooner.

I had my third mammogram one month after my graduation and this time, I had to return for a three-month follow-up. The radiologist informed me that the edges of the lymph node (seen in the previous films) looked different. I was petrified! Three months seemed like an eternity, but at the follow-up, the radiologist gave me a series of screenings and an ultrasound.

When it was time to receive my results, the radiologist shook my hand and said, "You're fine, and we'll see you in one year." Although I felt relieved, I still had a feeling that something was not quite right. I started to notice changes during self-checks at home. As much as I wanted to believe the positive reports, my gut feeling was that something was not completely right.

However, I quickly convinced myself that having two recent mammograms and ultrasounds meant everything was okay. I tried to erase all negative thoughts from my mind.

It was Women's Month at my church, and we hosted worship services every Friday night in May. On the second Friday night, the guest preacher appeared to have singled me out for prayer. In fear of the "floor ministry," I generally stay away from altar calls. I was standing at my seat, when the guest preacher bypassed the women at the altar, walked toward me, and prophesied very loudly in my ear. Just when I thought I was safe, she pushed me, and I began to fall awkwardly backwards toward the pew. I remember my backside ferociously hitting the front edge of the pew. I had a bruise the size of an iPhone 6 plus! The bruise was painful, but no comparison to the pain I began to feel in my lower back. Of course, I immediately associated the pain with the fall. *Why would God allow me to get hurt in church? After all, I was in church on a Friday night, worshipping and leading Women's Month.* I was baffled and confused. Meanwhile, the back pain continued for about one week.

> In fear of the "floor ministry," I generally stay away from altar calls.

Exactly one week after the fall, I was at work and started to feel progressively worse throughout the day. I decided to go home. I walked toward my car and attempted to sit in the driver's seat. As I attempted to sit down, I felt a pain radiate down my spine and then through my entire body, which prevented me from being able to sit completely behind the steering wheel. I stood in the empty parking lot of my job, clinging to my door for support, and looking around for a co-worker or just a friendly face to help me.

I was afraid. My husband was out of town at a conference and most of my family lives in Baltimore. I felt alone and frightened. I was in excruciating pain. I called two of my friends, Eric and Pat, who both agreed to meet me at Patient First. I prayed to God that He would allow me to somehow sit in my car and be able to drive myself to the doctor's office. God answered my prayer. I drove slowly and cautiously to a Patient First near my home, so that I would not be too far away from my children, who would soon be arriving from school. I realized that I had no range of motion and that every bump in the road felt like it would take me out!

Once I arrived at the doctor's office, I eased out of my car and dropped my keys. As I attempted to reach for my keys on the ground, I, at once, realized that I was unable to bend or move in any direction. Therefore, I kicked my keys into the office and signed myself in as quickly as possible. A kind lady asked if I needed help picking up my keys. With tears in my eyes, I informed her that I needed assistance. My back was hurting so terribly that I could not bend over.

When I heard my name, I walked slowly and methodically to the first triage area. I informed the nurse that I was unable to sit, so he took my pressure and temperature, as I stood against the wall.

Once I entered the treatment room, I was unable to put on the hospital gown on my own. An even more difficult task was lying flat on the X-ray table and moving into various positions for the pictures. The technician had to help me maneuver, because I was in too much pain to move independently. To my surprise, the X-rays showed that everything was fine. I had no fractures or no other obvious injuries.

> To my surprise, the X-rays showed that everything was fine!

The doctor informed me that based on the size and location of the bruise, I most likely had a severe muscle sprain. Her explanation seemed to make sense, so my only question was about managing the pain. The only time I could move on my own was to receive the shot for the pain! I leaned over the table and received a shot that would inevitably prove to be useless. Subsequently, I spent one week at home unable to walk without pain. It was very painful to sit and uncomfortable to sleep. I felt helpless and frustrated. I was also unable to bathe or get dressed without a great amount of discomfort and lower back pain. One day, I stood in the shower and just cried out to God for help. I could no longer take the pain or the state of helplessness. I was so accustomed to my independence. I quickly realized how much I took for granted.

It was difficult to mask my back pain, so everyone knew and offered a plethora of unsolicited medical advice. First, I sought help from my primary care physician. She looked perplexed, as I explained the pain and activities that I was no longer able to do without a significant amount of pain and discomfort. She prescribed Tramadol to "treat" the pain.

I thought if I lost weight, then perhaps my back would

feel better. I spent fifty minutes with my personal trainer, three times a week. We worked on low impact exercises, which would not exacerbate my back pain. We also worked extensively on stretching, because again, the assumption was that I had a severe muscle sprain with "tight muscles" from the fall. On Tuesdays and Thursdays, I worked out on my own, walking, working out in a swimming pool, and stretching.

One day, as I worked out in the pool to relieve my back pain, I met a kind, older man who appeared interested in my odd water workout. I explained my back injury to him, only to find out he was an orthopedic surgeon. He reassured me that the back pain was a result of my fall at church. He felt that my fall caused either a severe muscle sprain or a pinched nerve.

I then started physical therapy. I had heat applied to my lower back, completed a series of exercises, and then had the therapist massage the "injured" area. The heat offered temporary relief. However, the pain never completely stopped.

A well-meaning church member recommended a chiropractor. Out of desperation, I tried that too. After my initial consultation, the chiropractor taped my back and explained the course of treatment. The most perplexing issue I faced was that I had an extremely difficult time lying down, both on my stomach and flat on my back. I awkwardly lay face down on the chiropractor's table. First, he used a machine that sounded like a staple gun. Then, he manipulated the table in different directions.

During the very last manipulation, it felt as though the chiropractor had dislocated my back! I yelled out, and he stopped moving the table. I attempted to get off the table and soon realized, I could not move. I was in excruciating pain again and started to cry as I lay helplessly on the table. The chiropractor paced the floor, with his hand to his head. He repeatedly apologized and stated that he never had that happen to any of his patients. After fifteen minutes, with the chiropractor's help, I managed to get off the table and sit in a chair. It felt as if all of the strength had left my body.

I left the office and could barely open the door to my truck. Immediately, I called my husband to tell him about my awful experience. I was at my lowest point. I was tired of being in pain and so frustrated that nothing was working. I was no longer convinced all I had was a muscle sprain. Against my better judgment and the urging of family and friends, I returned to the chiropractor to "give it a chance to work."

The chiropractor continued to tape my back, and I think that the tape gave me some temporary psychological relief. However, one morning, I woke up only to realize I could no longer stand up straight. It was a scary moment. After about an hour, I was able to stand. However, every time I transitioned from a seated position to standing one (or vice-versa), I would feel a horrible pain in my lower back. There seemed to be a clicking sound accompanying every transition. It would temporarily immobilize me until the pain subsided.

I thought it was time for a visit with my doctor. My doctor was not immediately available. Therefore, I decided to visit the emergency room. Unfortunately, this would prove to be another worthless attempt to get better. Once I completed the check-in and triage process, I sat in a treatment room. An ER doctor entered the room, asked a few questions about my back, poked at it three times, and prescribed some hydrocodone. I asked him if I could have an MRI, and he informed me that the order for an MRI had to come from my primary care physician.

I returned to my general practitioner, this time armed with a letter. I listed every type of treatment and medication I had tried for three months. I expressed my frustration with being in pain and unable to lead a normal life. With every aspect of my life negatively affected, I desperately wanted help. I was unable to fully be a wife to my husband, and I was often too tired and in too much pain to be present, or available, for my children. I cried, prayed, cried some more, prayed, and just could not take it anymore!

> I was unable to fully be a wife to my husband, and I was often too tired and in too much pain to be present, or available, for my children.

I begged my doctor to order an MRI to find out what was really going on with me. At the same time, my friend, Tamara, a nurse, had already found an orthopedic specialist for me to see a few days later. (In retrospect, I realize that God had placed some awesome friends in my life, whose expertise and resources in the health field really helped when I needed it the most). When I gave this information to my doctor, she asked me to continue taking the pain medication and wait for the specialist to examine me and order the appropriate tests.

Finally, I made it to the orthopedic doctor, a back specialist.

I just knew that I would finally get some answers and start to feel better right away. The doctor asked me to reach to the floor, lean over to my left and right side, and then to lie flat on the table. None of which I could do! The doctor informed me that the only way to truly know the cause of my excruciating and debilitating back pain was to have an MRI!

After what appeared to be an eternity, I finally had the MRI, which was no small feat for my claustrophobia or difficulty lying flat for forty-five minutes. Fortunately, I was able to complete the screening, with the assistance of a compassionate technician who helped me get on and off the table.

The days leading up to receiving my results seemed long. My worse fear was that I would need back surgery. When I received the results from the specialist's nurse practitioner, I was extremely nervous. The moment of truth had arrived. I noticed that the nurse practitioner was seeing my results for the first time. I read the radiologist's report by peeking over her shoulder, as she cautiously explained the next steps. I think that the nurse underestimated my intelligence. I could see the words "hematologic workup," "bone scan," and "pathology" in my report. Then, I saw the phrase, "possible metastasis of the bone marrow." Immediately, I thought of one word—cancer.

> Immediately, I thought of one word—cancer.

It felt as though I could not breathe. The nurse informed me that I needed to have a bone scan as a first step, because I had two spinal fractures—one compressed and one sacral fracture. She asked if anyone in my family had osteoporosis. After this first question, I thought, well maybe I have osteoporosis. Then, carefully and with seeming ambiguity, she stated that cancer was a possibility. She said she had to mention it, because it needed to be ruled out.

Ma'am, what did you just say?

Next, she placed a box of tissues next to me, on the table, and stated, "I know this must be the worst day of your life." I became numb and confused. Why would this professional say something like that without giving me a diagnosis…no definitive answer to my pain? After all, she was not the actual specialist. She was just reading my results for the first time. Perhaps she missed something.

The specialist scheduled the bone scan and gave me another prescription for my pain. I asked about having a brace, but the doctor told me I would not need anything until after the scan. This made me nervous. I felt as though I could further injure myself and eventually, be unable to walk or move. On the contrary, I was reassured that I would be fine to go home.

I left the specialist's office in tears. I was scared. I sat in my car and immediately called my mother. Sometimes, we just need the comfort and listening ear of our moms. As soon as I heard her voice, I started crying, even more as I shared that I had two fractures in my back, which may have been caused by osteoporosis — or even worse — cancer. Instantly, she said it just couldn't be cancer! As much as I wanted to believe her reassuring words and

> Sometimes, we just need the comfort and listening ear of our moms.

hold on to her unrelenting faith, my gut feeling was that I was about to face some really tough days. I could not stop replaying the words of that MRI report in my head. Again, I turned to some of my friends who work in the medical field. I believe they did not want to alarm me and were hoping for a positive outcome.

Of course, my inquisitive nature did not stop with asking my friends, but I also had to do my own research. I've often heard that obtaining medical information from the Internet can be a dangerous thing. I quickly discovered why. Everything I read about bone scans and possible metastases included that dreaded word—CANCER. The more I read online, the more frightened I became over the next few days.

The more that I read online, the more frightened I became over the next few days.

On the day of the bone scan, I was extremely anxious and still in a great deal of back pain. My bone scan felt like I was lying on a conveyor belt with a low overpass, which was going to collide with my head! Once the scan was complete, I vividly remember the technician asking me, "What did you do to mangle your bones like this?" Again, I thought, I only had fractures from the fall at church. I thought my worst-case scenario would be to have back surgery to repair the fractures or perhaps I would need to wear an uncomfortable back brace. I was scheduled to receive the bone scan results on a Thursday in August. However, I received a phone call from the doctor's nurse, who asked me to come in one day early. I suddenly had a feeling in the pit of my stomach that something was wrong. However, I had no idea it was as bad as I would soon find out.

My husband and mother accompanied me to the doctor's office, for moral support. The doctor walked in and apologized for not being able to help me. He said that my back problem was "beyond the scope of his practice." He suggested I see an oncologist as soon as possible. He went on to say he had already set up an appointment for me with the same doctor who had treated his mother. He informed me that I had cancerous lesions throughout my bones, and it appeared to be a metastasized cancer. He stated that he had never seen "mets" like that previously. I sat silently on the table, as my mother and husband asked all of the questions. I specifically remember my mother asking the doctor where the cancer was located. The doctor seemed to name just about every part of my body! I could feel fear rising in my soul. I just didn't know what to expect.

What did my future hold? Was my prognosis grim? Why would God take everything away from me after giving me everything I had prayed and asked Him for? Would I have to endure chemotherapy? Surgery? Radiation? Unwanted weight loss? Negative side effects from medication? Hair loss? Nausea and vomiting?

On the ride home after receiving the cancer diagnosis, I sat quietly in the passenger's seat. My mother sat quietly in the back seat. I noticed that my husband was crying, as he drove us back home. I grabbed his arm and said, "I need for you to be

I grabbed his arm and said, "I need for you to be strong. We will get through this, but I need you to be strong."

strong. We will get through this, but I need you to be strong." In retrospect, I don't even know how I managed to think or speak those words.

As we got closer to home, I turned up the music in my car. It was a song called "The Benediction" by Anthony Brown and Group Therapy. The lyrics pierced my soul: *"Your hand is upon me, Your grace covers me, Your blood has washed me and I'm Yours totally."* I began to cry, not because I'd just been diagnosed with cancer, but because I was reminded of Whom I belong to! The first portion of Jude 1:24 states, *"Now unto Him that is able to keep you..."*

I felt a glimmer of hope.

My only request was to know the bare minimum. I did not want to know my prognosis, the stage of the cancer, nor anything that would serve to make my mental process more difficult to bear. (I didn't find out that my diagnosis was stage IV until I inadvertently saw it written on one of my forms as I signed in to see my doctor). My new medical team was formed. I had to visit another specialist who would perform a breast biopsy. I was petrified! I never felt comfortable with male doctors, especially for more private issues and concerns. However, I knew that I had to see the best practitioners. Because I felt let down by my previous doctors, I needed to, at least, try this new team.

My husband and mother accompanied me to the doctor's office again. I thought that he was only going to examine me, perhaps do an ultrasound and then schedule the biopsy. However, I soon discovered he was about to perform the biopsy right there in the office. I was not mentally prepared.

Many thoughts flooded my head. I felt like a piece of meat. *My breast will be scarred or disfigured, I thought. And what if the doctor couldn't find a tumor? What would that mean? How painful would the procedure be?* This would be my third biopsy. The other biopsies were uncomfortable but not painful. However, I never had anyone cut a piece of my breast. I felt perhaps my womanhood would be affected in some way. The doctor was very sensitive to my mental state and carefully guided me through each step. As my husband stood by the bed (holding my hand) and my mother sat in the corner quietly praying, the doctor proceeded.

First, he used an ultrasound machine to locate the tumor and to guide the procedure. I was alarmed at how quickly he found the lump. And, yes, I asked him how was he able to seemingly go right to the lump, which a mammogram and ultrasound, just three months earlier, could not detect. He had no answer. With the ultrasound tool in place, the doctor numbed the area where he would make the small incision. It wasn't too painful. He removed several samples and sent me home with an ice pack and a huge sense of relief, the procedure was now behind me.

My first visit to the oncologist was less than one week later. It was a difficult visit at the Virginia Cancer Institute. Being surrounded by other cancer patients, who appeared to be living with various stages of the disease, was hard. Most of the patients seemed to be much older than I. Some patients appeared quite frail and others were bald, most likely from chemotherapy. My husband held my hand as we entered the doctor's office. I have never been more frightened in my life.

The doctor entered the room and appeared to be very professional, listening to all my concerns. I explained to him that I was scared and only wanted to know what I *had* to know. I didn't want to know the stage of the cancer, nor any type of grim prognosis. He, yes, another male doctor, was very understanding and obliged my request. He then proceeded to inform me that he had reviewed my MRI, bone scan, and

My diagnosis was metastatic breast cancer.

biopsy reports. My diagnosis was metastatic breast cancer. He said that I had a malignant tumor in my right breast, which had metastasized.

I was beyond shocked, because I had just had my annual mammogram with an ultrasound, three months earlier. Oddly, I was relieved to know, finally, exactly what was going on with my body. I actually thought I had some type of lymphoma or leukemia. However, I had a cancerous tumor in my right breast, the same breast that I'd asked my gynecologist about, and the same one re-examined on my previous mammogram! The cancer had spread from my breast to my bones and liver. The cancer in my bones had caused the fractures observed on my MRI and bone scan. A CT scan showed cancerous lesions on my liver.

At last, I knew what was causing my debilitating back pain, yet I had no idea that it was the result of breast cancer. Why wasn't it detected earlier? I followed every precaution given to women my age. All I could think about was the statement that "early detection saves lives." *What about my life?* My cancer had already spread, only three months after having a mammogram and an ultrasound.

The doctor proceeded to explain that I would require chemotherapy, because the disease had metastasized. I was not a candidate for surgery or radiation. The doctor began to name the chemotherapy drugs I would receive, as well as the side effects I could possibly experience. As he listed the side effects, including mouth sores, dry mouth, discolored nails, and hair loss, I began to cry again. Mouth sores? How was I going to sing with mouth sores? I asked God to change it…and that is just what He did!

The doctor briefly left the office to check on something. When he returned, he stated that because of the type of breast cancer I had, he needed to change the drugs. The new combination did not include mouth sores as a side effect. This was the first very clear sign from God that I would not have to "battle cancer." That phrase really bothers me. We often hear people say of those with cancer, "They are battling cancer" or make statements like, "She/he has succumbed after a long battle with cancer." God won the battle of sickness on the cross (Isaiah 53:5). Therefore, I don't have to battle, I just have to believe!

Before I left the doctor's office, the oncologist informed me that if the disease had been caught earlier, I would have only had to endure hormone therapy. This really stung, because I had been seeking medical help since December 2014, for what I was told was a lymph node (which I could feel under my right arm). I was vigilant with my monthly self-checks, annual physicals, and my mammograms.

How could this have been missed?

The next difficult step was to inform my children who

were ages twelve, fifteen, and seventeen. They shed tears, but they were all very strong. My kids really stepped-up to the plate and helped me get through some tough days, both physically and emotionally. My main request was that they would not use my illness as an excuse not to do well in school.

All too often, I've seen many of my students use their family circumstances as an excuse to act-out and not do well in school. Even sadder, is the tendency for the adults to justify poor choices and awful study habits because of problems at home. Children need to be encouraged to focus their attention on school and to take their mind off problems, for the sake of their own future success. Fortunately, my illness did not affect my children's academics.

I had to have a port placed in my chest to begin chemotherapy. This process would begin some of the most difficult days of my life. I had the port placed in my chest at a surgical center not too far from my house. I entered the building with my husband and my parents. A nurse walked me to the back, where she gave me an IV, in a little room only separated from the other patients by a thin curtain. I could observe the nurses walking back and forth, from patient to patient. I wanted this to be a dream. Sadly, it was my new reality.

> I wanted this to be a dream. Sadly, it was my new reality.

The nurse entered my compartment and asked me some questions. I was startled to see my chart only listed "bone cancer" and not metastatic breast cancer. I inquired about this, and the nurse made the correction. I was not willing to allow any more mishaps with my medical care. The nurse apologized and told me I was too young to have that diagnosis. I agreed but quickly got a dose of reality.

The patient next to me, who appeared to be a woman in her late fifties or sixties, moaned and groaned during my entire stay. It was quite morbid in that little waiting area. The operating room nurse came to transport me to the OR. When I arrived at that cold room, everything in the room appeared to be alive. I felt like the instruments and even the people were out to get me. There were three nurses, two women and one man, who asked me to slide from the first table to the operating table. At that time, I was still in a great deal of pain. I could not move to the table on my own. I asked for help. The male nurse placed his arm under my back as the other nurses grabbed my legs under the sheet to roll me over to the operating table.

The surgical team draped and prepped me for the procedure. They informed me I would be asleep and, therefore, would not remember anything that happened. The nurse placed some medicine in my IV. I was still awake and very much aware of everything taking place. I could feel a tremendous amount of pressure in my chest. Fear overtook me, and I started to cry uncontrollably. I told the nurse I could feel everything, and I did not feel sleepy at all...not even groggy! She gave me more medicine. However, I was still alert. At this point, I had no trust in medical personnel. I felt betrayed and just like a piece of meat that was cut, without regard for how I felt.

Again, I asked God, *"Why?" Why would He allow this to happen to me? Was I a bad person? Did He not love me anymore? Was I being punished for my sins?* I just didn't know what to think, but I was heartbroken, confused, and in a great deal of pain. I had only mustard seed faith left and held on to it to make it through the next few days. The ordeal was finally over, and I went home to recuperate.

Over the next few days, I began to receive many phone calls and visits from concerned family, church members, and friends. I had to take a leave of absence from work, as I was unable to move or get around without pain. My mother and mother in-law took turns staying in my home to help me, assist with the kids, and to help around the house. I had pain medication administered around the clock, so they would come to my room at all hours of the night to bring me a small snack and my pain medicine.

During the first few weeks after my diagnosis, it was difficult to walk, especially up and down the stairs. I needed help with bathing and getting dressed. My husband and my mother in-law had to help me put lotion on my legs, because my range of motion was so poor. It hurt to bend over, and I became quite depressed. *Would I spend the rest of my life being so dependent on others for the things I previously took for granted? Would I be able to drive again or even ride in a car (the bumps and movement were quite uncomfortable)?*

My faith was put to the test and now, more than ever, I had to trust God. I had to rely on the words in those songs I had sung in church since I was eight years old.

On the night before I was to start chemotherapy, I suddenly became overwhelmed with so many emotions. I knew that my husband, my mother, and so many others were praying for me. But this time, I had to talk to God for myself! I threw some pillows on the floor next to my bed, and I fell on my knees. I wept and cried aloud! I didn't have a fancy "First Lady Prayer" (I don't even know what that would sound like!). I called on God, as if I was drowning in an ocean, and He was the only person that could save me. I called on Him that night, until I had no strength left, and all I could say was "God, help me!" I just stayed there until I had enough strength to stand and climb into my bed.

I sought the Lord, and He heard me,
and delivered me from all my fears.
—Psalm 34:4

When life presents you with a detour, it is great to have people interceding and praying for you. But at some point, you have to talk to God on your own behalf and tell Him exactly what you need.

Lessons Learned

• *Don't be too afraid to seek medical attention.*

• *Demand competent medical care and leave any practice that does not meet your needs.*

• *Be resourceful.*

• *Ask others to pray for you, but remember to talk to God for yourself!*

All I Know

All I know is that He knows the way that I take; when He has tested me, I will come forth as gold.

—Job 23:10 NIV

꧁꧂

CHAPTER 3

A Devastating Detour

For the thing which I greatly feared is come upon me,
and that which I was afraid of is come unto me.
—Job 3:25

The First Day of Chemo

I never wanted to have chemotherapy. It was the day I had dreaded—my first treatment day. I began what would be a weekly routine at the Virginia Cancer Institute. I had blood drawn and all of my vitals taken to monitor any changes or concerns. I entered the infusion room and was greeted by more compassionate staff members, all of whom made every effort to make me feel comfortable.

My oncology nurse explained each step, as I eased into the large, black chair in front of the nurse's station. My nurse sprayed numbing cream on the area where my port is located. Next, she inserted the IV needle into my port. It was painless. Various medications for nausea were administered and then, three different types of chemotherapy drugs. I was surprised to learn that there were different types and levels of chemotherapy drugs, with different side effects. I was blessed with a strong support team, family and friends, to accompany me to every treatment and/ or appointment. During the first hour of treatment, I sang songs with my sister to take my mind off of my new reality. The infusion center was full, every chair occupied. We sang softly to avoid disturbing any of the other patients. During the second hour of treatment, I became extremely restless and uncomfortable. I tossed and turned as the pain seemed to increase throughout my body. Fortunately, this would be the worst of my treatments, as I found a way to better manage the three-hour sessions.

After my first treatment, I didn't notice any side effects right away. However, after the second and third treatments, I became extremely fatigued. I had bouts of constipation, diarrhea, nausea, and overall malaise. I never lost my appetite; however, there were certain foods that I could no longer eat like citrus and spicy foods. As a native Baltimorean, this was difficult, because I love seafood and could no longer enjoy any of my favorite Old Bay seasoned dishes. I also love grapefruit, oranges, and strawberry lemonade. But during treatment, I had to stop consuming many of my favorite dishes and snacks. After my third treatment, I started feeling even more nauseous, though I had not vomited.

One morning, my awesome husband decided to make breakfast for me. The food was good, but that was the morning I discovered that citric acid was no longer my friend! I started eating my delicious breakfast and minutes later, I vomited all over our bedroom. I felt awful. I didn't want my husband to think that his cooking had made me sick. Fortunately, I would only vomit one additional time (after drinking some lemonade). Otherwise, I didn't lose my appetite during treatment and as a result, I never experienced a dramatic weight loss. I could no longer use regular toothpaste because it burned my mouth. I had to buy a specialized toothpaste and mouth rinse during treatment.

In addition to the chemotherapy, I had to get two shots every month. The first shot, which was given to strengthen my immune system, caused an awful joint and muscle pain! I felt trapped in my own body, unable to move without pain. The second shot was given to strengthen my bones. This shot only hurt when being administered—OUCH! Eventually, I became used to being stuck repeatedly. Although the regimen was tough, I knew that it was working, because I started to feel better and slowly regained my range of motion. Even though I never experienced a dramatic weight loss, I did lose my hair—all of it.

Losing my hair hurt me deeply. I was fond of my coal black bob and my husband—my high school sweetheart—had always loved my hair. I noticed that my hair started to shed, so I got it cut. I always had relaxed hair, so for the first time, I fell in love with my natural

Losing my hair hurt me deeply.

curls. Unfortunately, my hair continued to shed more and more every day. Between my second and third treatment, my hair came out in clumps. For some reason, I thought it would stop and I'd be able to keep my black soft curls.

One day, I noticed that after trying to manipulate my hair, it was really coming out even more. So, I decided to go to the hair salon. I thought I would get it washed and cut even closer. However, after shampooing my hair, my stylist informed me that a lot of my hair had come out in the sink. When I looked in the mirror, I saw that I was completely bald on my crown. My stylist suggested I just shave my head completely and I agreed, because I knew that it would all come out. I began to cry because I felt like I was losing a part of my identity and myself. I felt ugly. I was worried about how my husband would feel. I did not want my children embarrassed by how I looked. It was so hard!

My mother and my daughter were with me. My daughter said, "Mom, it really doesn't look that bad. I think that you look pretty." My mother sat in a chair next to me and had the other stylist cut her hair as a sign of solidarity. They both uplifted my spirit, along with my stylists, who were extremely professional and compassionate. I made the decision to just be bald and not wear wigs. Wigs just didn't work for me, as they were uncomfortable and hot! I decided to just accept myself and not worry about what others thought of me. Fortunately, my husband had no problem with my new look. He made a statement that touched my heart. He said, "I'd rather have a bald wife than

> I decided to just accept myself and not worry about what others thought of me.

a buried wife. We will do whatever we have to do to get you better."

Over time, as more people learned about my diagnosis, I received some very interesting gifts. It appeared that every gift and card related to breast cancer. I started to dislike the color pink and ribbons! I prefer not to be defined by my condition. One day, I received two "Breast Cancer Bibles." I thought, "I'll just stick to the King James Version!"

I quickly learned that everyone handles tough situations differently. Although I think most people had well-meaning intentions, I was not in a mental state for receiving, what I call, "breast cancer paraphernalia." When I didn't receive pink blankets and ribbons, I was asked very personal questions about the disease, stage, and my treatment plan. I used to be profusely private, which is hard to do when you grow up in the church and then marry a preacher!

I used to be profusely private, which is hard to do when you grow up in the church and then marry a preacher!

My husband made a videotaped announcement for our congregation, which played during a weekend that we were away with some friends. We knew that questions would be asked, especially when I walked to the pulpit the next Sunday to sing with the praise team, now sporting a bald head! In lieu of answering some of the questions that made me feel uneasy, I decided to document my treatments and share my journey on social media. This was a therapeutic way for me to manage my reality and simultaneously share my experience with others.

As much as I wanted to remain private, I knew I had to educate others and spread the word to my sisters, to advocate for quality healthcare. Although my original doctors and mammography seem to have failed me, my gut instinct and determination to find out what was going on with my body may have saved my life.

> When your body tells you that something is wrong, it is important to listen!

When your body tells you that something is wrong, it is important to listen! Don't wait! It's okay to be afraid. I was very afraid. Yet, I also knew that I wanted to grow old with my husband and watch my children grow into successful and prosperous adults. So, I did everything possible to find out what was wrong and how I could fix it.

(Get your mammograms! Ask for an ultrasound, and demand an MRI. Get your annual physicals and do self-checks at home. Know your body!)

In addition to interrogations about my condition, I often received unsolicited testimonials. Many people (again…I am sure they mostly had great intentions) shared their cancer stories, whether their own or the plight of living, or even dead, relatives who were diagnosed with cancer. This became even more frustrating than questions about my condition. Some people would tell me about the awful side effects, suffering, and many times loss of loved ones from cancer. These types of stories frightened me and caused my mind to wonder to some very dark places.

For months after receiving my diagnosis, I could not sleep. I stayed awake every night. No matter how hard I tried, I just could not fall asleep. My pain medication helped me to feel comfortable, but it did not help me to sleep. I talked to my doctor about my insomnia, and he prescribed some sleeping medication, with a stern warning about the possibility of addiction and too much dependency on the medication for sleeping. With much hesitation, yet desperation, I tried the sleeping pills and still found myself only averaging about three to four hours of sporadic sleep each night.

> Some nights, I'd simply watch my husband sleep and think about how much I love him... how I wouldn't want to leave him or my children.

I often thought about my harsh reality. I closed my eyes tightly and hoped that my diagnosis was just a bad dream. Some nights, I'd simply watch my husband sleep and think about how much I love him...how I wouldn't want to leave him or my children. Most nights, I would pray and ask God to help me get through the next day. I would ask Him to help me to think on positive things and not to be so pessimistic and sad.

Every three months, I have a CT scan for my doctor to observe the state of the original tumors and lesions. The scan also allows my doctor to make sure that there are no new malignancies. In order to prepare for the test, I stop eating for four hours before the test. I also have to drink flavored barium sulfate, which always makes me feel nauseous. At the clinic, I have blood drawn first and then I lie on the CT scan table. A technician places an IV in my arm and the machine, operated by another technician in a separate room, begins to scan my entire torso. The solution in the IV is released, giving a warm sensation throughout my body. A few more pictures are taken to complete the scan and then, I return to my doctor after a few hours to get the results.

Getting the results for my scans is always an unnerving experience. My first CT scan confirmed the cancer. The next scan revealed that the chemotherapy had shrunk the cancerous tumors and lesions and that God was working! I was so thankful for the positive reports.

Although the treatments were rough on my body, I also noticed that my back pain had finally subsided. What a relief! I was starting to feel something, which I had not felt in a long time—HOPE. A cancer diagnosis feels like a death sentence. However, I was determined to live and to live happy.

Lessons Learned

- *Listen to your body.*
- *Be thankful for great doctors and medical professionals who allow God work through them to give you quality health care.*
- *When confronted with your worst fear, it is okay to cry and to be angry (just don't stay in that miserable place for too long).*
- *Believe in miracles!*
- *Embrace who you are, embody your journey, and inspire others with your story.*

All I Know

All I know is that I shall not die, but live,
and declare the works of the Lord.
—Psalm 118:17

◈◈

CHAPTER 4

I Feel Like a Virgin!

Love is patient, love is kind.
—1 Corinthians 13:4

My treatment had one side effect that my oncologist did not prepare me for. Cancer affected my sex life! At the beginning of my diagnosis, I was in a great deal of pain. Quite honestly, I think that my husband was afraid of hurting me. I was afraid too. It was mentally nerve-wracking to know that I had fractures in my back. For several months, it hurt to sit, stand, walk, or lie down. So, any type of exercise, especially lovemaking, just seemed to be out of the question. However, my desire to be intimate with my husband never wavered during my sickness.

Of course, we had to think of some creative ways to enjoy *that* part of marriage. Yet, I quickly learned that sex isn't the most significant part of a healthy marriage. My husband was extremely patient and never pressured me or made me feel like his needs weren't being met. Actually, I had a more difficult time with this unwanted "drought" than he did.

After one of my early treatments, I was able to convince my husband to, at least, try *it*. I felt like a virgin. My body had not physically caught up with my emotions. Sex wasn't painful, but it just didn't feel like it did before my diagnosis. Some of the medications I was under caused me to have early menopause-like symptoms. I was diagnosed with the type of breast cancer that is primarily estrogen-induced. Therefore, early menopause was part of my treatment plan.

I felt worthless. I could not please my husband the way that I wanted to, as a woman in my forties, and it made me very sad. I felt like he deserved so much more than what I was able to give him. I shared this with him and as we both shed tears, he reassured me that sex was not a priority for him at this phase of our relationship. He wanted me to be well, healthy, and whole again.

So, we had a special kiss throughout my chemotherapy sessions. Every hug was intense. We no longer took any touch, word or look for granted. I fell in love with my husband in the tenth grade and twenty-eight years later, I love him even more than I ever thought possible. When God gives you a gift, there's nothing like it!

> Every hug was intense. We no longer took any touch, word or look for granted.

We went five months without sex, yet we experienced the most powerful intimacy ever (in our almost twenty years of marriage). The quirks, which, from time to time, bothered us and caused tension or disagreements, now seemed silly. I wish every married couple could experience this level of intimacy in their own marriage, the magnitude of appreciation my husband and I have for each other, and our level of loyalty (yet, without having something like cancer as the catalyst for authentic marital bliss!).

Lessons Learned

- *Life challenges shift your priorities.*
- *Marriage is bigger than sex.*
- *Intimacy is much better than sex.*
- *Appreciate your spouse and treat every day as if it were your last day together. (I guarantee that you won't go to bed mad about dirty socks or farts ever again!)*

All I Know

All I know is that nothing or no one can separate what God has joined together.
—Mark 10:9

CHAPTER 5

A Divine Destiny

Many are the afflictions of the righteous:
but the Lord delivereth him out of them all.
—Psalm 34:19

I have experienced the miracle of healing, yet I still have so many questions about my journey. I don't want to miss any lesson from this divine detour.

I can't help but reflect on the many miracles Jesus performed in the Bible. From sermons, Sunday-school lessons, and Bible studies over the years, I've learned about so many instances in the Bible of people who suffered, encountered Jesus, and received a miracle. In many of the stories, we learn all about biblical personalities who experienced suffering and pain. We then learn how they overcame their issue with God's help.

For example, in Matthew 9:18-26, we read about the woman with the issue of blood. We discover that she suffered for twelve years, but she became whole after touching Jesus. Within the same story, we learn about how God revived Jairus' daughter because of this man's faith. Jesus also raised Lazarus from the dead and healed the ten lepers. We read about their miracles, but there is no written account of what occurred days, months, or years after these miracles. I wonder if the woman with the issue of blood had days or just moments where she feared that she would start bleeding again. Did Jairus' young daughter live with the fear of dying again?

> There is a thin line between faith and fear.

As thankful as I am for my healing, there are still moments when the fear and reality of my condition overwhelms me. With any physical pain, I wonder if the cancer has returned or become worse. Then, I feel a tremendous amount of guilt, because I feel like I place my fear ahead of my faith in God. There is a thin line between faith and fear.

In addition to the physical and mental struggle, I also deal with the emotional aspects of my miracle. During the days after my diagnosis, I was inundated with visitors, phone calls, cards, ribbons, cancer Bibles, free dinners, extra kisses, and hugs. I had house guests who helped me take care of my children and my home. But over time, the calls and visits lessened. Suddenly, I felt a strange sense of loneliness. Although I still had a core group of supporters, it just didn't feel the same. The expectations of what I should now be able to do were overwhelming. Even though the worse days of cancer are behind me, there are still days when I feel exhausted and unable to perform at the level I did before cancer ravaged my bones.

I returned to work, but I was still in treatment and felt exhausted every day. Any type of housework seemed to bring back that nagging ache in my side and my back. For the most part, I kept this to myself, because I didn't want anyone to think I was being lazy or getting sick again. And I certainly don't want pity…ever!

I push through the pain and fatigue. When I know that I need to stop and rest, I just sit down somewhere. I want to be the best wife and mother possible. More importantly, I want God to be proud of me. I know that He will always be with me and carry me through every situation.

Lessons Learned

- *Challenges show you who your real friends are.*
- *When people walk away, God will still be with you.*
- *Fear does not come from God.*
- *Mustard seed faith can overcome a mountain of fear.*
- *Know when to get rest and be still.*

All I Know

All I know is that some trust in chariots, and some in horses: but I trust in the name of the Lord our God.
—Psalm 20:7

Beloved, think it not strange concerning the fiery trial which is not to try you, as though some strange thing happened unto you: but rejoice, inasmuch as ye are partakers of Christ's suffering; that when His glory shall be revealed, ye may be glad also with exceeding joy.

—1 Peter 4: 12-13

CHAPTER 6

Divine Side Effects

And we know that all things work together
for them who love the Lord.
—Romans 8:28

I hate cancer. Yet, in a strange way, I think my diagnosis was divine. In many ways, I benefitted from my journey. First, it strengthened some important relationships that were either on life support or just not as strong as I would have liked.

My husband and I have always had a strong relationship. Neither one of us believes in yelling, cursing, or being disrespectful. The smallest things would often irritate us though, but in order to avoid conflict, we would "let things slide." That is until we were fed up! Then we would get everything off our chest and exist silently, until one or both of us was ready to move forward and be "regular" again. We were experiencing one of those moments of not being "regular" to the point that we were considering counseling just to get back on track. I learned that

God is the ultimate Marriage Counselor.

On that initial drive home from the doctor's office, I could feel how deeply my husband loves me, as he drove with tears streaming down his face. I was too numb to cry, but the thought of leaving him crushed me. In an instant, I observed the fragility of life and meaninglessness of my pet peeves and proclivities.

I wanted to spend every second with my husband. Not as pathetically as I did when we were first married and had no life of my own. Now, there was a genuine desire to be in his space and spend time with my best friend. I wanted to recant all of those silent treatments, which I thought had been so expertly executed over the years.

My illness also enhanced my relationship with my mother. For the first time, I fully understood that she still sees me as her child, despite my age. The love I feel for my children helped me to relate to how she feels. But experiencing her care, as an adult, totally gave me a new perspective. She sacrificed time away from her own house to make sure that my family and I had every need met. She cooked, chauffeured, and chaperoned. She prayed, cried, and celebrated every small victory.

I specifically remember the day I received the news from my oncologist that my treatment was "overwhelmingly positive." As my husband and I sat in the parking lot giving God thanks, the first person I called, again, was my mother. As I told her the doctor's report, before I could finish, all I could here was a resounding "Thank you, Jesus! I knew that You were gonna do it!" Well, this praise lasted for about thirty minutes, before my mother got back on the phone and said, "So, what else did the doctor say?" Parents are gifts from God, and I'm thankful that I didn't have to endure this journey without my mother by my side.

My diagnosis also reunited three of my closest friends and me. We all attended high school together and were roommates in college. Although we never stopped being friends, I think that time and distance kept us apart. Instead of taking the initiative to reach out to them and simply let them know I missed them, I remained quiet. I no longer have this problem.

Once they found out that I was diagnosed with cancer, each one of them, two doctors and a nurse, reached out to me. I was so overwhelmed and full, because I really missed our friendship. We planned a weekend together. It was so much fun! We laughed, ate, sang, and of course, played spades! We looked at pictures and reminisced about our high school and college days. Isn't it amazing how God can take something awful like cancer and make it bless your life?

> Isn't it amazing how God can take something awful like cancer and make it bless your life?

I had my posse back!

As I reflect on that weekend, I'm sure that they all probably knew more about my diagnosis than I did. At that time, I still didn't know the stage of the cancer. However, they were all very caring and discreet. It's a blessing to have lifelong friends.

In addition to strengthening relationships, this detour seems to have also given me a fresh dose of courage. From swimming, to flying, to something simple like crossing the street, I realized that I didn't have to be afraid. After all, I've encountered my biggest fear, which was cancer! I ask myself, "What can possibly be worse than a stage four cancer diagnosis at age forty-two?"

What are you afraid of? Have you encountered it? If so, what do you have to lose in confronting some of your other fears? If you have not encountered your worst fear, the good news is that God has already given you the victory!

Perhaps the biggest act of courage, for me, was reaching out to my mentor, Karen Clark Sheard. I've been a fan of her music since I was twelve years old. I used to have concerts listening to all of my Clark Sister's records (and yes, I had the album covers all over my wall)! I would sing all of her parts in my brush and practice her runs and riffs every day.

Now, thirty years later, I've had the opportunity to meet her and become her friend. I shared my diagnosis with her, and she called to have prayer with me! I will never forget that moment. It meant so much that she would sacrifice time from her busy schedule to pray for me. I kept her posted throughout my treatments, and when I became much stronger, I spent an entire weekend with her.

God, is this really happening?

Have you ever admired someone so much and finally had an opportunity to meet him/her and he/she exceeded your expectations? Well, that weekend was one of the best times I ever had...EVER! She was gracious and one of the sweetest, most genuine people I've ever met. We ate, talked, shopped, and of course, worshipped together! It was so much fun and I was tickled pink. Again, God took something ugly like cancer, and turned it into an opportunity of a lifetime!

But thanks be to God! He gives us
the victory through our Lord Jesus Christ.
—1 Corinthians 15:57 NIV

In all things we are triumphantly
victorious through Him who loved us.
—Romans 8:37

For God has not given us a spirit of fear,
but of power and of love and of a sound mind.
—1 Timothy 1:7

He who began a good work in you will carry
it on to completion until the day of Jesus Christ.
—Philippians 1:6

And that's all I know!

CHAPTER 7

The Advantages of a Detour

Saul became still more afraid of him, and he remained his enemy the rest of his days. The Philistine commanders continued to go out to battle, and as often as they did, David met with more success than the rest of Saul's officers, and his name became well known.
—1 Samuel 18:20-30

Forrest Gump's mother taught him "life is like a box of chocolates…you never know what you're going to get." I think this statement resonates with most people. Because most of us, no matter how well thought-out the plans have been in our lives, eventually, we each discover life can take us down roads we never thought we would travel.

If someone would have told me ten years ago, five years ago, or even one year ago, life would be as it is right now, I would have laughed or given that person a piece of my mind! But the truth of the matter is, life has a way of flipping on us.

Life has a way of changing. Life has a unique way of messing-up the great plans we once so meticulously planned.

> Life has a unique way of messing-up the great plans we once so meticulously planned.

The detour, or unexpected occurrence, is not always a bad thing, sometimes the *shift* is a good thing. My cancer diagnosis was horrible, and I would not wish that on anyone. However, my condition shifted some relationships and gave me a new perspective on life. It gave me a new appreciation for simple things, which I used to take for granted (like driving to my favorite donut shop for a cup of hot cocoa or getting my hair done). A cancer diagnosis had always been my biggest fear, but I've discovered purpose in my pain. I learned that my experience is not a punishment, but a way to trust God, strengthen my faith, and to inspire others.

Love who you are, without worrying about what other people believe they know about you. Learn to live with life's challenges, which have become your new "normal."

But whatever you do, live!

Do it with joy and with a peace of mind. Every day you get up, face the new facts of your life and have a new resolve that says:

Things did not work out as I thought they would. I am not in the place I thought I would be and/or doing the thing(s) I thought I would be doing. But I'm still here!

You must declare, *I'm still alive! I'm still grinding! I'm still pressing! I'm still moving forward! I'm still kickin'! I'm still making noise! I'm still in the game! I still believe that God is in control of my life and my times are in His hand!*

The fact that you and I are still here simply means: God is not through with us yet! You should find comfort in those words because they are words of truth and hope. Yes, they are words of truth because, every now and then, you have to remind the people around you that you are not perfect. Yes, I'm saved. Yes, I attend church. Yes, I sing on the choir. I may even work in my church, but don't get it twisted, *God is still working on me!*

Sometimes, before you allow people to place you on a pedestal that is higher than the reality of your faith journey with God, you may need to remind them, "Don't do it...because I'm still under construction." God is still working on me. He's not through with me yet!

There are still areas in my life that I'm struggling with. There are still some habits I'm trying to break. There are some desires I wrestle with daily. God and I are still negotiating some things. Please don't judge me or place me on a level I have yet to attain. He's not through with me yet!

That's another word of truth, but it's also a word of comfort. May I prophesy to you today? Whatever you are going through...whatever you are confronted with now...whatever the insurmountable situation in your view...whatever the challenge...I want you to know that God is not through with you yet!

I believe what God said in Jeremiah 29:11:

For I know the thoughts that I think toward you,

saith the Lord, thoughts of peace and not of
evil to give you an expected end.

Don't you give up!

Don't you quit!

Don't throw in the towel!

Don't you walk away!

Don't make any funeral arrangements!

Don't roll over and die…and you better not…give in!

Because friend, He's not through with you…this is just a detour!

In fact, God might just be using you to show somebody else how to deal with his or her detour! The detour isn't even about you anyway. God might be using you to show somebody else that you can go through something hard and still have joy, still live a good life, still be able to walk in your church and declare, "This is the day that the Lord has made, I will rejoice and be glad." You have to have that radical "Job talk" that says, *"Though He slay me, yet will I trust Him!"*

Please do me a favor. Close this book for a moment, and open up your mouth and scream as loud as you can…*God is not through with me yet!*

Sometimes what the enemy uses to destroy you is the very same thing God will use to develop you. I believe that most of us are the product of some type of detour. There was something we had to fight through or something that we had to live through. There was something (or someone) we had to discover how to live without. There were some disadvantages, challenges, situations, or obstacles, which made it difficult for us to make it through. Yet a situation that may have destroyed others, God could be using to develop you. You must discover ways to finagle your way through this detour. I will tell you how you can make it. This is what you must do, get up every morning and keep moving forward...

Whatever the disadvantage...get up and keep moving!

Whatever the challenge...get up and keep moving!

Whatever the obstacle...get up and keep moving!

Whatever the handicap...get up and keep moving!

Whatever the situation...get up and keep moving!

Whatever the detour...get up, square your shoulders (ladies, put on some lipstick and get your nails done), and keep it moving!

When you consider the life and times of David, you will recall Saul wanted him dead. He wanted to destroy him. He devised a plan and attempted to take David out. But sometimes what your enemy thinks will erase you, is the very same thing that God will use to establish you. Saul had a strategic plan of placing David on the front line of the battle, believing David would die in the battle. However, Saul forgot that David was a warrior. Fighting was David's specialty!

Friend, when you live with a detour, you have to rely on the things that work best for you. The worst thing your enemy can do is to back you up into a position where you have a proven success rate. Your enemy will make a mistake if he affords you the opportunity to get in your zone. You are a force to reckon with when you're in your zone. You can handle any test when you're in your zone. You win when you get in your zone!

I don't know what is challenging your future trajectory, but whatever it is, push past it and get in your zone! Stop complaining and get in your zone. Stop worrying and get in your zone. Stop talking about what you can't do and what you can't handle...and what you can't get through...*get in your zone!*

This is not your obstacle. This is not your first test. This is not your first storm. She/he is not the first difficult person you've met. This is not your first breakup. This is not the first time you've had to deal with bad news. Get yourself together and get in your zone! Believe it or not, your detour is making you a star!

Don't miss the lessons of your divine detour. Whether you're a cancer survivor, like me, or living with another challenging experience, just remember, God will never leave you.

He's right there!

I was young and now I am old, yet I have never seen the righteous forsaken or their children begging bread.
—Psalm 37:25 NIV

Yep, that's all I know!

CHAPTER 8

Delighting in the Detour

A cheerful heart is good medicine.
—Proverbs 17:22

Throughout my journey, I've shed many tears. But I was always uplifted by laughter! Now, I thoroughly understand the proverb that laughter is the best medicine.

A few days after my diagnosis, my husband and I spent a weekend at a bed-and-breakfast, with six of our closest friends. We had the best time. It was the first time I could smile after receiving the devastating news. It felt great to laugh again and to forget about my pain.

Sometimes therapy comes through laughter.

Some of the laughter came from a group of friends who sent text messages every day. I don't like talking on the phone, but I love to read text messages! I had one friend, Akin, who sent me weekly videos with a full comedy routine to cheer me up throughout chemo. I had friends send messages just to check-in, and it kept me going.

When was the last time that you made someone laugh? You never know how you can turn someone's day around by simply smiling and being kind. Even at the cancer clinic, I was able to laugh. From the phlebotomists, to the technicians, to the nurses, I found comfort in their smiles and friendly personalities. My doctor's medical assistant, Ms. Priscilla, always makes me laugh. She gives a firm hug and is always able to bring my pressure down on stressful days, through laughter.

In addition to laughing, I noticed that I felt better when I looked good. If you're reading this book and you hate makeup, at least wear some Vaseline and clear nail polish! Fix yourself up. Get those eyebrows tweezed or waxed (right now). You don't have to look like what you're going through.

I'll never forget my first day of chemo. As I was getting dressed, I was just going to throw something on and skip my usual makeup routine. However, my husband looked at me and said, "I want you to be the most beautiful person in that infusion room. Show the other patients what it looks like to beat this thing!" That's exactly what I did. I did my make-up and put on the cutest comfortable outfit I could find. My best accessory was a smile, because I knew that I wasn't alone and that the infusion center wouldn't be the end of my detour.

At the beginning of my illness, I could barely walk. For a short while, I had to walk with a cane, a leopard print cane, but a cane nonetheless! That was rough but necessary. I had to sleep on a mountain of pillows (literally) and I had to ride in my car with pillows. I had to use a step stool to get in and out of my bed and in and out of my truck. Over time, I was able to get through these moments with love and laughter. I also did my best to look like an over-comer, instead of looking defeated.

I don't know where this detour is going to end. All I know is that I feel better physically, mentally, and spiritually. I've regained the ability to do some of the things I could do before my diagnosis.

Yes, I can do *that* again too!

All I know is that the thing I dreaded the most invaded my body, but I'm still standing! I know that God won a battle I couldn't fight alone. He blessed me with a loving husband, great children, and supportive family, friends, and colleagues. God sent many angels to pray and intercede on my behalf.

From a tedious Ph.D. program, to a grueling sickness, God has shown me who He is and what He is able to do when my only option is to trust in Him. I pray you, too, will have the audacity to put your trust in Him. God can handle anything! Nothing you experience, including cancer, is too big for God. Just tell Him about your detour, then sit back, and let Him guide you toward your destiny.

> God can handle anything! Nothing you experience, including cancer, is too big for God.

No matter what your detour is, just remember Ephesians 3:20:

Now unto to Him that is able to do exceeding
abundantly above all that we ask or think,
according to the power that works in us.

Now, that's *really* all I know!

About the Author

Taleshia L. Chandler has worked in education for over twenty years. She is passionate about learning and understanding how people think and learn. She serves as the first lady of the Cedar Street Baptist Church of God, where her husband, Anthony, is the senior pastor. Taleshia enjoys singing and sharing the good news about Jesus Christ and His awesome healing power. After being diagnosed with metastatic breast cancer in August 2015, Taleshia is determined to spread awareness about appropriate cancer screenings and patient advocacy.

Taleshia received a bachelor's degree in psychology from the University of Maryland Baltimore County. She earned a master's degree and Ph.D. in educational psychology from Walden University. She resides in Glen, Allen, VA with her husband, Anthony Sr. and their three children, Anthony II, Alysha, and Andrew.